"The Art of Living the Happily Depressed Life"

A Story of Embracing the Light Within the Shadows

By Ankur Raj

Self-Published
Edition Year: 2024

Copyright Page

Epigraph

"We discover the rhythm of being, not perfection, in the interplay of light and shadow. Living completely means embracing the darkness's subtle knowledge rather than chasing it away." - Ankur Raj

Foreword

Life often feels like a series of contradictions: joy and sorrow, light and darkness, success and struggle. Yet, in the midst of this duality, there lies a profound truth—we are not meant to eliminate the shadows but to find harmony within them.

In The Art of Living the Happily Depressed Life, Ankur Raj fearlessly grapples with the labyrinth of depression and mental health, providing his readers with a deeply personal yet widely relatable journey into what it means to live authentically. A student in his undergraduate years, Ankur writes with the lucidity and candor of one who has, if nothing else, seen life's turbulent storms and learned to walk through them graciously with reflective introspection.

This book does not promise easy solutions or impossible ideals; it asks readers to sit with their emotions, love vulnerability, and find beauty within quieter moments in life. Through practical tools, heartfelt anecdotes, and profound wisdom, Ankur takes us on a journey of self-discovery and acceptance.

Reading through this book is as if you are sitting down with your friend who truly gets how you're hurting and reminding you that it is fine to feel. It is a testament to the strength found in softness, the resilience born from heaviness, and the quiet joy hidden in simplicity.

I feel that this book will speak profoundly to anyone looking to navigate the complexities of their emotions in life, reminding them that sometimes within life's grayest days, light lies in wait.

Preface

When I started writing "The Art of Living the Happily Depressed Life", I wasn't looking for answers, but rather trying to hold on to the questions. Life is inherently an up and down affair. We are socialized to chase happiness, and often sit still quietly with sadness. This book came out of the introspection of this journey in search of those contrarian points in life.

Being an undergraduate, I have known the bright hope of youth as well as the crushing weight of doubt. Like many others, I wrestled with what the world told me to fix myself, to conform into a representation of happiness. But increasingly, over the passage of time, I realized that true healing came not from fighting darkness but from learning to coexist with it.

This is not an antidote to depression or a recipe for permanent happiness. Rather, this is an invitation to appreciate the beauty of something imperfect, to notice little joys which pass us by, and to celebrate the light and the dark together as two sides of the same whole.

Through this work, I have tried to articulate the nuances of living authentically amidst life's challenges. The practices and reflections I share are drawn from my own experiences and the wisdom I've gathered along the way. My hope is that this book will resonate with anyone who feels lost, heavy, or misunderstood, reminding them that even in the quietest moments, there is strength and light to be found.

Thank you for choosing to come on this journey with me. I hope these pages bring you comfort, connection, and the courage to embrace your own beautifully complex life.

— Ankur Raj

Acknowledgements

To everyone who helped and encouraged me to write "The Art of Living the Happily Depressed Life", I sincerely thank you. You are the cornerstone of this work, people who have faced their own challenges and told their tales of resiliency.

I also thank the quiet times of meditation, the gray clouds of life, and the paradoxes of human feeling that have led my pen. Your presence taught me the beauty of imperfection and the strength in vulnerability.

This book is dedicated to all readers who find a piece of themselves within its pages. I hope it serves as a reminder that light and dark may coexist harmoniously and that we can actually learn to live by accepting both.

Introduction

What does it mean to live a "happily depressed" life? On the surface, the idea sounds paradoxical—in a way, even contradictory—because how is it possible for depression and happiness to coexist? But this paradox was exactly what motivated me to write this book. In a world that seems to celebrate constant cheer and perfection, those of us who live with depression are often left feeling broken or misplaced. We are constantly being "cheered up" or "stay strong" as if we were problems unto which a solution needed to be found. But what if we stop trying to fix ourselves and instead learn to live fully with all our imperfections intact? This collection of reflections, tools, and stories opens up perspectives on the art of finding harmony in life's contradictions. It does not promise quick fixes or a cure for depression; instead, it offers an invitation to sit with your feelings, honor your vulnerabilities, and uncover the quiet joys that can exist even on the darkest days.

We will examine these practices in mindfulness, journaling, reframing perspectives, as we explore how to navigate the heavy emotions of navigating happiness and finding peace in the silences that we perhaps try so hard to avoid. Together, we will look at how embracing life's paradoxes might lead to a more authentic, meaningful existence.

I don't have all the answers—far from it. But what I do have is an open heart and a willingness to share what I've learned along the way. My hope is that this book becomes a companion for you, a reminder that it's okay to feel deeply, to struggle, and to grow at your own pace.

Welcome to this journey of living the "happily depressed" life. It may not be perfect, but it's real—and that's enough.

— Ankur Raj

Contents

Chapter 1

The Comfort of the Gray Clouds

The world oftentimes suggests that happiness is the goal, the golden standard of a life well-lived. But to some, happiness does not equate to perpetual sunshine; it is gentle gray skies. It has to do with an open consideration of days that do not have to shine bright and clear.

The grey clouds of life remind of old familiar friends who come and go. They bring with them, in every time of its presence, a type of quiet reflection that only overcast skies can bring. For those navigating depression, such clouds are not really a signal of doom. This familiarity might be the grounding factor during the bad times.

The secret to working with these clouds is to learn how to sit with them, feel their weight without judgment. Just as the rain nourishes the earth, melancholy truly nourishes creativity, empathy, and introspection.

Even though it is small, its sustenance is substantial. We learn endurance and tolerance from life's grey skies. They demonstrate that not every moment must be bright in order to have significance. They ask us to pause, reflect on our lives, and find beauty in imperfection and simplicity in their silence.

The calm force of introspection is often overlooked by society, which frequently associates greyness with stagnation or melancholy. The most transforming times might be when we feel most confined. These times force us to slow down, focus on our inner selves, and re-establish connections with aspects of ourselves that are frequently obscured by the bustle of everyday life.

Grey skies invite us to accept the present and let go of the demands of never-ending work. They serve as a reminder that growth need not necessarily be obvious or loud; it can unfold subtly, like a plant sipping from a gentle rain.

Lessons from the Gray:

(1) Acceptance Rather Than Resistance :
Acceptance is the practice of learning to sit with the grey clouds. We might compassionately lean into these emotions rather than fighting against melancholy or trying to push ourselves into happiness. Acceptance is realising that each emotion has a role and a purpose in our life, not giving up.

(2) Discovering Meaning in Silence :
The grey clouds serve as a reminder of the importance of calm in a culture that frequently exalts

busyness. We can examine our feelings and thoughts in peace during these quieter times. Personal development and deep insights can result from this reflection.

(3) Perspective as a Gift :

Similar to how grey skies offer a neutral background that amplifies the world's brightness, depressing times can deepen our appreciation of life's most joyful moments. We could never really comprehend appreciation or joy without contrast.

Here, we explore practical exercises in finding comfort in the storms of life: mindfulness practices to journaling emotions just as they are without any attempt to change them.

Here's how to embrace the clouds:

(a) Sit at a window on a cloudy day and practise mindful observation. Take note of how the grey makes the scenery seem softer. Note how it reflects your feelings.

(b)Everyday Grey Reflection:
At the end of the day, consider times when the "grey" gave you the opportunity to stop, reflect, or establish a deeper connection with oneself.

(c)Gratitude for Overcast Days:
Make a list of the things in your life that you are thankful for, even if they are quiet, such as a reassuring habit or a favourite book.

(d) Mindful Rainy Days:
The next time you see a cloudy day, sit by a window and observe the rain or go on a walk in the drizzle. Take note of the calming cadence of the droplets and the way the dim light alters your surroundings. Allow the scene's serenity to permeate your mind.

(e) Create a Ritual:
Create a cosy routine for grey days by wrapping yourself in a favourite blanket, lighting a candle, or brewing a special tea. These small deeds might become into emblems of comfort and self-care.

An Insight into Change :
The impermanence of grey clouds, both real and metaphorical, is one of their most comforting characteristics. As storms pass and are replaced by sunlight, so too do difficult periods in life come and go. We can handle these times with patience and hope if we are aware that they are fleeting.

But long after the clouds clear, the lessons they leave behind frequently endure and improve our lives. We learn to appreciate not only the sunny summits but also the darkened valleys along the way from grey clouds.

Remind yourself that it's acceptable to feel muted while you welcome the grey sky. Taking a break from aiming for eternal happiness is acceptable. Light and shadow coexist in harmony in life, and both are necessary for our development and comprehension. Grey clouds are comforting because they quietly reassure us that beauty, purpose, and the possibility of fresh starts can exist even in the midst of the silence.

Chapter 2

When Happiness Is Too Loud

It's easy to feel alienated in a society screaming, "Be happy, be positive, be productive!" when, ostensibly, it seems that all of life's joys are at an arm's length. This chapter delves into the overwhelming pressure of forced positivity.

Happiness can also be loud-beaming smiles and grand proclamations of success. But for those quietly navigating depression, happiness doesn't arrive with confetti-it's a faint flicker, a soft whisper in the chaos.

This chapter challenges us to embrace ourselves, flaws and all, instead of telling our inner voices, "I'm okay." We learn how to counter the kind of poisonous positivity that cloaks itself in positive thinking as we transform the notion of success, moving away from a phantom world of perfect images and towards being livingly authentically.

We should "stay positive" at all times, according to toxic positivity. This counsel might feel damaging and alienating to people who are dealing with depression.
The "louder is better" theory of happiness is contested in this chapter. It's acceptable to feel alienated by calls for optimism all the time. Genuineness is more important than fake joy.

The Illusion of Perfect Happiness :
The concept of toxic positivity, which holds that we should always be happy, simplifies the human experience into a flat, one-dimensional story. It disregards the importance of feeling the whole range of emotions, the complexity of emotions, and the certainty of battle.

Pop culture and social media frequently portray happiness as loud, glitzy, and performative. It's the well-curated Instagram image, the beaming party smile, or the outspoken assertion of achievement. However, that isn't often how true happiness appears. Many people find that happiness is elusive—a little moment of calm, a single breath of comfort in the midst of chaos—especially those who are silently navigating the depths of sadness. It's the dim gleam of a star on an overcast night, not the fireworks.

The Damage of "Good Vibes Only" :

The phrase "good vibes only" may seem positive, but it can have serious negative effects. Instead than acknowledging and processing negative feelings, it suggests that they should be avoided or repressed. Phrases like "Just stay positive" can come out as arrogant to someone who is already struggling, as if their suffering isn't accepted or legitimate.

This method encourages shame in addition to invalidating genuine feelings. You may begin to feel like you're failing at life and at being human if you're not content or productive. And the cycle of loneliness and self-doubt may be exacerbated by that assumption.

Embracing Authenticity Over Perfection :

Adopting sincerity is necessary to combat poisonous positivity. It's about accepting our emotions, whether they be fear, rage, sadness, or joy, without passing judgement. Real development and healing result from confronting our feelings with compassion and honesty rather than from acting as though nothing is wrong.

Redefining Happiness :

It's not necessary for happiness to be extravagant or noisy. It can be found in the little things, like the comfort of a well-known song, the warmth of a cup of tea, or the silent fulfilment that comes from doing a straightforward work. We make happiness more approachable and less dependent on social norms when we broaden our definition to encompass these small pleasures.

The Power of "It's Okay" :

We can practise saying "It's okay not to be okay" rather than making ourselves say "I'm fine" when we're not. This small change makes room for self-compassion and vulnerability. It serves as a reminder that sometimes it's sufficient to just sit with our emotions; we don't always need to make all the changes right away.

Practical Steps to Counter Toxic Positivity :

(a) Permission to Be Real:
Create a list of emotions you feel but hesitate to express. Practice saying them aloud, even if just to yourself.

(b) Finding Quiet Joy:
Instead of going to a loud event, try to find delight that is in line with your energy, such as listening to a soft music.

(c)Pushing Back Against Toxic Positivity:
When someone tells you to "just cheer up," practise saying something nice but forceful. For instance, "I'm processing my feelings in my own way, but I appreciate your intention."

(d) Set Boundaries with Positivity Pushers :
It's acceptable to keep your distance from people or situations that constantly encourage you to feel bad about your feelings. Express your desire for space to process your feelings in a genuine way in a polite but strong manner.

(e) Seek Genuine Joy :

Instead than focussing on what society says should make you happy, consider what actually makes you feel comfortable or satisfied. This could be redefining success according to your own standards or taking a vacation from social media.

We might question our ideas of success by rejecting the "louder is better" view of enjoyment. It is not necessary for success to be a glittering, well-publicized accomplishment. Finding moments of calm in the middle of stress, learning to control your emotions, or practicing self-compassion can all be subtle and intensely personal.

We regain control when we give ourselves permission to define success and pleasure as we see fit. We discover how to value our individual paths and accept the whole, messy, lovely range of human experience.

Authenticity is the cure to toxic positivity, not negativity. We create space for something much more satisfying when we let go of the urge to be consistently happy or well-groomed: real connection, profound self-awareness, and the silent strength that comes from accepting ourselves just the way we are.

Chapter 3

The Myth of Fixing Yourself

According to self-help culture, we should always work to "fix" ourselves, but what if we're already whole? The idea that being "whole" entails not experiencing sorrow or hardship is debunked in this chapter.

We are frequently made to believe that happiness is a destination—a polished, glossy version of ourselves that we must continuously work toward—in the unrelenting turbulence of self-help culture. As though our current selves are insufficient, we are constantly inundated with advice to "improve" and "fix" what's wrong with ourselves. What if we're not broken, though? What if we accepted grief and adversity as necessary components of our wholeness rather than as flaws?

Rather, it reinterprets despair as a special perspective on life rather than as a flaw. The chapter offers examples of how accepting flaws can increase resilience and self-awareness.

This chapter reframes hardship and hopelessness as distinct perspectives on life rather than as defects. It clarifies the misunderstanding that happiness equates to perfection and shows that real healing involves accepting grief as a natural part of life rather than trying to eradicate it.
We're not broken puzzles in need of fixing. The myth that happiness lies in perfection creates a relentless cycle of dissatisfaction. True healing isn't about eliminating sadness but living with it as part of the human experience.

The Myth of Perfection :

A never-ending cycle of discontent is produced when people think that reaching a perfect state of being is the key to happiness. We say to ourselves, "I'll be happy when I get that job, lose that weight, or fix that part of me I don't like." When those objectives are accomplished, however, the joy is short-lived, and the cycle restarts. We end up chasing an illusion in this drive, failing to see the worth in our current selves, flaws and all.
Integrating flaws into our sense of ourselves is what true wholeness is all about, not hiding them. It's about realising that grief, adversity, and vulnerability are not obstacles to happiness but rather paths to introspection and development.

The Wisdom of Kintsugi :
Kintsugi, an old Japanese art form, provides a powerful metaphor for this way of living. Gold is used to fix broken ceramics in kintsugi, highlighting rather than concealing its cracks. Not in spite

of its past, but because of it, the restored item gains beauty and value.

Consider using this theory to treat emotional injuries. We can accept our challenges as a part of our story rather than ignoring or concealing them. Similar to how kintsugi's golden seams draw attention to the vessel's journey's beauty, our wounds and hardships can reveal the depth, resiliency, and power of who we are as people.

Useful Kintsugi Techniques for Emotional Recovery

(1) Rethinking Emotional Injuries :

Think back to a challenging time in your life. Think about how it has shaped you rather than seeing it as something to be erased. What connections, insights, or strengths have resulted from it? We turn our wounds into signs of development when we view them as sources of knowledge.

(2) Expression of Creativity :

To "golden-line" your own emotional journey, use writing, art, or another creative activity. Make a written or graphic record of your challenges and successes that highlights the beauty in your flaws.

Getting Rid of Perfectionism :

Letting go of perfectionism is a prerequisite for embracing our totality. The idea that we need to be "fixed" before we can be happy breeds incessant self-criticism and unrealistic expectations. Alternatively, we can approach self-improvement with a more realistic and caring mindset.

(1) Realistic Self-Improvement Goals :

Adopt understanding as the objective instead than perfection. For example:

Rather than stating, "I'll be happy when I'm successful," attempt, "Today, I will take one step towards understanding what success means to me."

Instead of saying, "I need to fix my flaws," say "I'll learn how my imperfections shape who I am."

(2) Focus on Process, Not Outcome :

The journey, not the goal, is where happiness and development can be discovered. You can find fulfilment in the process of becoming by concentrating on tiny, important tasks, like keeping a journal, taking care of yourself, or getting help.

Vulnerability's Strength :

Vulnerability, which can be unsettling or even frightening, is necessary for us to accept our imperfections. However, self-acceptance and genuine connection are predicated on vulnerability. We make room for recovery and development when we show our flaws to dependable loved ones or even simply to ourselves.

Redefining Healing :

Erasing sadness or reaching a state of perfect bliss are not the goals of true healing. It's about recognising that happiness and sadness belong together and learning to live with the whole spectrum of human emotions. Similar to kintsugi, healing includes recognising the beauty found in our imperfections, respecting the narratives they convey, and deriving significance from the patchwork of our life's events.

We are not broken vessels that need to be repaired or riddles that need to be solved. Despite our wounds and cracks, we are already complete. We can move away from the draining quest for perfection and towards a better, more genuine experience of life by accepting our flaws. Happiness comes from realising that we were never broken in the first place, not from trying to cure ourselves. Our golden seams—the difficulties we've encountered and the fortitude we've developed—are what really make us lovely, much like kintsugi.

Chapter 4

Embracing the Art of Feeling Heavy

Depression frequently makes you feel as though you are carrying an unseen burden that pulls at the borders of your spirit. This chapter explores how that weight can serve as an anchor for you even though it might be draining.

Depression frequently feels like an invisible burden weighing down on the boundaries of your spirit, dragging you into a silent, lonely emptiness. It's simple to see this weight as something that should be resisted or fought. But what if this weight might act as an anchor rather than an enemy? What if, although being difficult, weight gave you a chance to stop, think, and re-establish a connection with yourself?

The idea of emotional gravity—a metaphor for the burden of depression—is examined in this chapter. Emotional gravity can bind us to the here and now, encouraging us to slow down and appreciate quiet, much like physical gravity holds us rooted to the ground. We can learn to deal with depression's weight in a graceful and resilient way by redefining it as a grounding force rather than a destructive one.

It's not necessary to be defeated to feel heavy. It might serve as a prompt to slow down, take a break, and reconsider. We talk about the idea of emotional gravity and how to accept the weight without allowing it to break you.

The Dual Nature of Heaviness :
Being heavy need not be a sign of failure. It might be a reminder to take a break, examine your inner life, and rebalance your emotions. Heaviness, like a tree's roots, can keep you grounded during emotional storms so you don't get carried away by the mayhem. This viewpoint recognises depression's contradictory capacity for stability and insight rather than downplaying its difficulty. In order to manage the weight with grace and tenderness, this presents grounding practices including sensory mindfulness and creating safe zones. The weight of depression can feel crushing, but it can also be grounding. Like roots holding a tree firm in a storm, heaviness reminds us to pause.

Practical Strategies for Navigating Emotional Weight:

1. Using Sensory Mindfulness to Ground Oneself:
When emotions feel too much to handle, grounding exercises can help you stay grounded and provide a sense of stability. These exercises remind you of your present-moment existence and place

an emphasis on connecting with your physical environment.

Techniques:
(a) Ground to Foot Awareness:
Keep your feet flat on the ground while you sit or stand. Feel how the ground supports your weight and is firm beneath you. "I am here, and that is enough," you can say out loud or mentally. Continue saying this until you feel in control.

(b) The 5-4-3-2-1 Technique:
Name five things you can see, four things you can touch, three things you can hear, two things you can smell, and one item you can taste using the 5-4-3-2-1 technique. By bringing you into the present, this sensory exercise helps you decompress from racing thoughts.

2. Slow Motion Meditation :
The mental rush that sadness frequently imposes can be effectively countered by slowness. You can change your attention from the weight in your head to the feelings in your body by moving slowly and deliberately.

Practices:
(a) Slow Stretching:
Start with easy stretches like touching your toes or raising your arms above your head. Feel every muscle relax and lengthen. Take a deep breath and move in unison with it.

(b) Mindful Walking:
Take your time and focus on each step. Take in your body's rhythm and the feel of the ground beneath your feet. This technique helps reduce emotional burden by fusing mindfulness with physical exercise.

3. Redefining Heavy Days :
It's acceptable that not every day will be light. Bad days can be a reminder to take a break, refocus, and take care of yourself. Think of being heavy as a notice from your body and mind to take a break rather than as a failure or a setback.

Journal Exercises to Encourage Reflection:
(a) What might my heaviness be telling me?
(b) How can I use this time to care for myself?
(c) What small actions can I take today to feel supported or nurtured?

You can regain control over your emotional experience by accepting and recognising difficult days without passing judgement.

4. Creating Safe Zones
Having a defined "safe zone" might offer consolation and confidence when feeling heavy becomes too much to handle.

Ideas for Safe Zones:

(a) A Physical Space:
Decorate a comfortable area of your house with blankets, soft lighting, and cosy objects. When the world becomes too much to bear, let this place be your haven.

(b) A Mental Safe Zone:
Imagine a location that makes you feel safe, like a beach, a forest, or a memory from your early years. Make use of this mental picture as a haven when things get tough.

5. Self-Compassion During Difficulties
Self-critical thoughts are frequently brought on by a significance level, but it's crucial to handle these situations with empathy. Show yourself the same consideration that you would a friend.

Affirmations for Difficult Times:
(a) "It's okay to feel this way. I am doing my best."
(b) "This weight does not define me; it's just a part of my journey."
(c) "I will move through this at my own pace."

Discovering Power in Silence
Even if depression is challenging, it also invites you to take it leisurely and get back in touch with yourself. It promotes silence, which is conducive to reflection and recovery. Sitting with and navigating heaviness can help you become more resilient and self-aware, just like roots grow deeper during storms to keep a tree sturdy.

Being heavy can ground you rather than break you. You can turn the weight from a burden into a tool for stability and growth by intentionally leaning into it. Depression may push you, but it can also serve as a reminder of your resilience, strength, and presence—much like the ground beneath your feet.

Chapter 5

The Beauty of Small Joys

Happiness is frequently found in the simplest, most underappreciated moments; it's not necessarily a big gesture. Readers can learn how to develop an appreciation for the small things that make life livable, even beautiful .

Joy isn't usually extravagant or theatrical. It frequently resides in the little, underappreciated moments of daily existence—the little things that, even in trying circumstances, provide warmth and comfort. However, these small pleasures are easy to overlook in a society that exalts great accomplishments and landmarks. This chapter examines how developing mindfulness and an appreciation for life's more subtle joys may change your viewpoint and make even the worst days brighter.
Joy frequently lurks in plain sight, whether it's in the way sunshine filters through a curtain, the rustle of leaves in the breeze, or the first taste of tea in the morning. Even on the worst days, you can discover moments of joy by slowing down and learning to notice these brief moments.

Rediscovering the Beauty in the Everyday
Like sunlight leaking through a crack in the curtains, true joy frequently enters subtly. It's in the little, fragile details:
(a) The aroma of freshly brewed coffee in the morning.
(b) The soothing rhythm of rain tapping against the windowpane.
(c) The comforting embrace of a favorite sweater.
(d) The first bite of a delicious meal after a long day.

These apparently unimportant moments are the threads that make up a life of peaceful satisfaction. It can be a deep exercise of mindfulness and self-care to learn to appreciate and acknowledge them.

Journaling about thankfulness, exploring the senses, and making a "joy jar" to hold tiny reminders of beauty are examples of useful activities.

Happiness doesn't always arrive as fireworks. Often, it sneaks in like sunlight through a crack in the curtains.

Practical Practices to Embrace Small Joys :

1. Joy Journaling

Spend a few minutes every night writing down one small item that made you happy during the day. It doesn't have to be remarkable; it may have been the sound of laughter with a buddy or the crispness of the morning air.

Why It Works....?:

You can educate your mind to look for and value the little things by thinking back on these experiences. This exercise has the potential to change your viewpoint over time, enabling you to find beauty in everyday tasks.

Quick Examples:

(a) What was the most comforting moment of my day?
(b) What made me smile today, even briefly?
(c) What sensory experience stood out today—something I tasted, smelled, or heard?

2. Creating a Joy Jar

A joy jar serves as an apparent indicator of the small pleasures in life. Put a little piece of paper in the jar and write down anything that makes you happy, such a nice phrase, a humorous memory, or a stunning sunset.

How to Apply It:

(a) On difficult days, revisit the jar and pull out a note. Reliving these happy moments can provide comfort and perspective.
(b) Over time, the jar becomes a tangible collection of gratitude and joy.

3. Mindful Appreciation

You may completely experience and appreciate the little pleasures that are frequently overlooked when you practise mindfulness, which enables you to savour the present.

Simple Practices:

Before Reading:
Take a deep breath and appreciate the weight of the book in your hands or the feel of the pages.
Before Eating:
Pause to admire the colors, textures, and aroma of your meal. Reflect on the effort that went into preparing it.
Before Sleeping:
Lie down and take a moment to feel the softness of your pillow or the warmth of your blanket.

Senses as an Entrance to Happiness

Our senses are excellent resources for joy and for interacting with the outside world. We can find satisfaction in the here and now and ground ourselves in the present by consciously interacting with them.

Ideas for Sensory Exploration:

Sight:
Watch sunlight dance through leaves or notice the colors in a sunset.
Sound:
Listen to birdsong, wind rustling trees, or your favorite music.
Smell:
Inhale the scent of a flower, a candle, or freshly baked bread. Taste: Savor a piece of chocolate, a warm cup of tea, or a ripe fruit.
Touch:
Feel the texture of a soft blanket, cool water, or a loved one's hand.

The Quiet Power of Small Pleasures

The fireworks of life—great accomplishments, extravagant parties, or large gestures—do not always equate to happiness. Frequently, the calm times are what keep us going:
(a) The way a pet greets you at the door.
(b) The satisfaction of finishing a good book.
(c) The warmth of the sun on your face during a walk.

Even the most routine day may be transformed into an incredible one by changing the focus from what is lacking to what is present.
You build a foundation of happiness that is independent of outside events when you learn to appreciate and value life's little joys. These small pleasures serve as pillars, supporting you during the highs and lows of life.

Joy does not necessarily come from making bold claims or throwing lavish parties. It frequently whispers, concealed in the sound of leaves rustling, the first sip of coffee in the morning, or the warmth of socks on a chilly day. You allow joy to be a continuous companion, subtly brightening even the darkest pathways, by turning your attention towards these moments.

Chapter 6

Friendship with the Void

The dark, empty area that sadness frequently produces, known as the void, might seem like a terrible foe. However, what if it isn't? What if it's just misinterpreted?

The void, a shadowy, empty place created by despair or sadness, frequently feels like an unwanted, stifling guest. However, what if the emptiness isn't necessarily harmful? What if it's actually a stop, a place that encourages change and relaxation, rather than a void? This chapter reinterprets emptiness as a partner to be understood, a teacher in disguise, rather than as an adversary to be defeated.

A wide chasm that threatens to devour happiness and purpose, emptiness can feel overwhelming. However, there is a call to stop and think amid its serene depths. When all distractions are removed, the emptiness forces us to be with ourselves and face what really important. We can learn to live with the emptiness rather than fight it, turning it from a place of fear into one of opportunity.

Befriending the emptiness is encouraged in this chapter. Sit with it, converse with it, and learn about its nature rather than resisting it. The emptiness frequently prompts us to stop and consider what is really important.

Techniques to Befriend the Void

1. Name It
The emptiness can become less abstract and frightening if it is given a name or identity. Instead of seeing it as an external opponent, you build a relationship with it by personalising it.

How to Do It:
(a) Imagine the void as a character or presence. What would it look or sound like? Is it calm and quiet, or loud and chaotic?
(b) Write a letter to the void, expressing how you feel about its presence in your life.
(c) Invite it to "speak back" by journaling as though the void is responding. This exercise can help you uncover hidden emotions or insights.

for example :
Dear Void, you feel heavy and endless, but maybe you're trying to teach me something. What do

you want me to learn?

2. Reframe Its Presence

The emptiness frequently resembles a loss or a lack of anything. By rephrasing it, you can perceive it as a place of relaxation, a break between the chapters of life.

How to Reframe:

(a) Think of the void as a room rather than a vacuum. A room can be empty yet comforting, offering space to breathe and regroup.
(b) Consider it as a cocoon, where transformation takes place slowly and quietly. Just as a caterpillar rests before becoming a butterfly, we, too, can use emptiness as a stage for growth.

Affirmation Technique:

(i) This is not the end; it's a pause.
(ii) The void is giving me space to rebuild.

3. Guided Visualization

By using visualisation, you can change your perspective of the emptiness and transform it into a secure and supportive environment.

How to Practice:

(1) find a quiet place where you can sit comfortably.
(2)Close your eyes and imagine the void as a dimly lit room. It's not cold or harsh; it's soft and still.
(3)Picture yourself entering this room and sitting in its center.
(4)Imagine the room holding you gently, offering a space to rest. Feel its quiet embrace.
(5)When ready, visualize a door opening, leading to a brighter, calmer place. This symbolizes the end of your time in the void and the beginning of a new chapter.

You can change the void's power dynamic by imagining it as a concrete, unthreatening area. Instead of swallowing you, it turns into something you can step into and out of.

Living with the Void

1. Journaling Discussions
You can communicate with the void by keeping a journal. Imagine if it has feelings, thoughts, and even suggestions for you.

Prompts:

(1) What does the void want me to know about myself?
(2) What is the void teaching me about what I truly value?
(3) If the void could speak, what would it say?

2. Grounding Practices for the Void

Although the emptiness can be unsettling, grounding techniques assist you in being in the now.

(a) Deep Breathing:
Sit quietly, breathe in for a count of four, hold for four, and exhale for six. Repeat until you feel calmer.
(b) Sensory Awareness:
Focus on your surroundings—what you see, hear, smell, touch, or taste. This anchors you in the present moment.
Mantra:
"I am here, and I am enough".

3. Transforming Heavy Days

It's not necessary to feel overwhelmed every day in the blank. Take advantage of these chances to think and start over.

Steps:

(a) Accept that heavy days are part of the cycle. They're not failures but signals to rest.
(b) Write about what the heaviness might be trying to tell you. Is it asking you to slow down? To let go of something?
(c) Treat yourself with extra kindness—watch a favorite movie, take a warm bath, or simply nap.

The Void as a Growth-Catalyst

The void can be a place of creation rather than a destructive force. It provides countless opportunities, much like a blank canvas. You have the opportunity to consciously rebuild when life seems stripped bare, choose what to keep and what to let go of.

Reflection Exercise:

Write down three things you've learned from your moments of emptiness. How have they changed your perspective or priorities?

Despite its intimidating nature, the void is not an enemy. It's a place—a silent, essential break in the pace of life. You may change it from a source of fear to a source of wisdom and fortitude by becoming friends with it, paying attention to it, and finding calmness inside it. The emptiness is a beginning, not the end.

Chapter 7

Laughing While Crying

Sometimes the only way to deal with the ridiculousness of life is to laugh through your tears. The healing potential of humour in the face of suffering is examined in this chapter.

We frequently encounter situations in life that are so perplexing, contradictory, or ridiculous that the only way to deal with them is to laugh. Although humour may seem far or subdued to people dealing with depression, it is still a potent tool—a link between pain and comfort, heaviness and lightness. This chapter examines how laughter may be therapeutic, even when tears are around.

Depression alters what you find humorous, but it doesn't take away your ability to laugh. We'll examine how absurdity, irony, and dark humour can be used as coping mechanisms.

Readers develop a sense of humour that recognises their challenges while easing their emotional burden by sharing personal stories and helpful advice. Contradictions are typically the source of life's ridiculousness. It can be therapeutic to laugh while crying.

The Paradox of Humor and Pain

Your sense of humour may change as a result of depression, but it remains intact. In actuality, humour frequently changes in reaction to adversity, becoming more profound, incisive, and meaningful. It creates moments of relief in the midst of the storm by enabling us to face life's absurdities without becoming overwhelmed by them.

Contradictions are the foundation of absurdity in life and are the breeding ground for irony, black humour, and absurdity. We can laugh because of our suffering rather than in spite of it when we acknowledge and accept these paradoxes.

The Healing Power of Laughter

(1) Laughter as a Stress Reliever
Laughter lowers the stress hormone cortisol and causes the body's natural feel-good chemicals, endorphins, to be released. The burden of depression may be lessened, however temporarily, by this dual effect.

(2) Humor as Perspective

Finding the humour in challenging circumstances reframes them rather than diminishes their gravity. By establishing emotional space, humour can assist us in taking a step back and better processing our emotions.

(3) Connection through Shared Laughter

Even in difficult times, connection is cultivated through shared laughter. Whether it's connecting over a humorous anecdote or finding comfort in a joke that speaks to us, humour serves as a reminder that we're not alone.

Techniques to Find Humor in Hard Times

1. Seek Relatable Humor

Look for comedians, events, or books that deal with subjects that are important to you. When conventional jokes don't work, dark humour, satire, or weird comedy can strike a deep chord.

For Examples:
Watching shows like The Office or Fleabag that explore awkwardness and vulnerability with wit. Reading comics or memes that exaggerate everyday struggles in hilariously relatable ways.

2. Create Your Own Darkly Funny Narrative

It can be therapeutic to write humorously about your difficulties. Making a joke or story out of pain doesn't make it any less real; rather, it gives you back some control over it.

How to Try It:

(a) Compose a poem or short tale about a difficult time in your life that has an ironic or exaggerated twist.
(b) Think of your difficulties as a stand-up act. What would be the lines of humour?

Prompt:

(a) "The time I tried to be productive while crying into my coffee..."
(b) "Why depression makes me the best weather forecaster (spoiler: it's always gray)."

3. Laughter Meditation

Your attitude can be surprisingly affected by even forced laughter. Embracing laughter as a method of mindfulness is what laughing meditation encourages.

Steps:
1.Find a quiet, comfortable space.
2.Begin by smiling, even if it feels unnatural.
3.Gradually let your smile turn into a laugh. Start small—just a chuckle—and build up to a belly laugh.
4.Observe how your body feels: the movement of your chest, the release of tension, the flow of air.

5.Allow yourself to laugh for as long as feels natural, even if it's tinged with tears.

Your brain may be tricked into releasing endorphins by the physical act of laughing, even if it is forced. It gets simpler to laugh in a genuine way over time.

Embracing the Absurdity

The most humorous parts of life are when things are contradictory.
Contradictions are typically the source of life's absurdity:

1.The universal struggle of misplacing your glasses when they're on your head.
2.Feeling utterly broken yet laughing at how relatable a meme about procrastination is.
3.Crying over a heartfelt commercial while eating an entire pizza—because why not?

Finding humour in these contradictions humanises them rather than trivialises them.

Transform Pain into Creativity

Even the most depressing moments can give rise to playfulness.
For example:
1.Create a humorous "depression bingo" card: squares could include "forgot what day it is," "answered a text two weeks late," or "cried because the soup was too salty."
2.Write mock product reviews about your experience with depression, e.g., "Depression: 1/5 stars. The emotional weight is too heavy, but at least it's consistent."

When Laughter Meets Tears

Laughter and tears are frequently two sides of the same coin. Both are strong emotional outbursts that can occasionally occur at the same time. Although it may seem paradoxical, allowing yourself to laugh while crying is one of the most common human emotions. It serves as a reminder that happiness and suffering may coexist.

The goal of humour in the midst of sorrow is to embrace the whole range of human emotion, not to minimise or reject your suffering. You assert moments of lightness in the midst of gloom by laughing at the unusual patterns of life. You'll discover that humour doesn't take away the burden of life, but it does make it a bit easier to bear when you learn to laugh through your tears.

Chapter 8

The Strength in Softness

Although society frequently exalts stoicism and toughness, there is great power in being vulnerable and allowing yourself to feel deeply.

Toughness and stoicism are frequently praised by society as the pinnacles of strength. However, real bravery is letting yourself be exposed—to feel deeply and honestly. Vulnerability is a powerful source of inner resilience, healing, and connection rather than a weakness to be concealed. This chapter examines the transformational potential of accepting vulnerability and offers practical strategies for using it to your advantage.
Vulnerability is redefined in this chapter as an act of courage. Being vulnerable to your feelings gives you the ability to connect with people and yourself in a genuine way.

Redefining Vulnerability as Strength

Letting your inner world be visible is what it means to be vulnerable. It involves recognising your humanity, flaws, and vulnerability to suffering. Ironically, being more transparent might help you and other people connect on a deeper level. Accepting vulnerability means letting go of the appearance of perfection and entering an environment that fosters development, empathy, and real connection.

Vulnerability Connects:
By showing your authentic self, you give others permission to do the same, creating relationships based on trust and mutual understanding.
Vulnerability Heals:
Expressing your emotions—whether through conversation, art, or reflection—helps release internal tensions and fosters emotional clarity.
Vulnerability Strengthens:
Facing your fears, doubts, and insecurities head-on builds resilience and a deeper sense of self-awareness.

We'll look at ways to use your tenderness as a strength through techniques like keeping an emotional journal, embracing artistic outlets, and sharing your vulnerability in a safe way with friends you can trust.

Although vulnerability is sometimes confused with weakness, it actually serves as a powerful source of strength.

Practical Ways to Embrace Vulnerability

1. Emotional Journaling: The Power of Reflection

One of the most effective ways to manage emotions and acquire new perspectives is to write down your ideas and feelings. You can face your vulnerabilities in a private, secure setting without worrying about being judged when you keep a journal.

How to Start:
Set aside 10 minutes daily to write without censoring yourself.
Use prompts like:
1.What am I afraid to say out loud?
2.What emotions am I carrying today? Why?
3.What would I tell my closest friend if I weren't afraid of being judged?

By externalising your feelings, journaling helps you feel less overwhelmed by them. It can eventually show trends and assist you in identifying your emotional triggers.

2. Art as Vulnerability: Expressing the Inexpressible

When words cannot adequately convey your feelings, artistic expression provides a special means of doing so. Making art facilitates the externalisation of emotions in a way that is both intimate and universal.

Artistic Outlets to Try:

Painting or Drawing:
Use colors and shapes to represent your emotions. For example, you might paint stormy skies to reflect inner turmoil or soft pastels to express calm.
Writing:
Craft a poem, story, or song inspired by your emotions. Whether it's raw and unpolished or carefully composed, the process can be cathartic.
Music or Dance: Create a playlist that mirrors your mood or let your body move freely to express what you're feeling.

Through art, you can express feelings in ways that are both meaningful and safe since it transcends language. If you feel prepared, sharing your creations with others can strengthen bonds as well.

3. Real Talk: Sharing Your Truth

Although it can be frightening, opening out to a loved one or trusted friend is one of the most brave displays of vulnerability.

How to Begin:

1.Choose someone you trust deeply, who listens without judgment.

2.Start small. Share one thought, feeling, or concern rather than diving into everything at once.
3.Use "I feel" statements to express yourself clearly and authentically. For example: "I feel overwhelmed by..."

Relationships are strengthened and your burden is lessened when you talk about your feelings. Being vulnerable serves as a reminder that you are not alone and frequently evokes empathy and camaraderie.

4. Creating Safe Spaces for Vulnerability

Vulnerability does not exist in any situation or relationship. By identifying and creating safe spaces, you can explore your feelings without worrying about being judged or rejected.

Steps to Create Safe Spaces:

Physical Spaces:
Find a quiet, comforting place where you feel at ease, such as a cozy corner at home or a serene park.
Emotional Spaces:
Establish boundaries in relationships. Be selective about who you share your vulnerability with—choose people who demonstrate empathy and respect.
Internal Safe Space:
Develop self-compassion. Practice speaking to yourself with kindness, as you would to a friend, even when you feel exposed or afraid.

Both physical and emotional safe zones offer a starting point for examining your emotions and developing self-assurance in your openness.

The Myths About Vulnerability

1."Vulnerability is Weakness."
Being strong means confronting and growing from pain, not avoiding it. Being vulnerable is having the courage to be who you truly are, even when it makes you uncomfortable.

2."Being Vulnerable Means Losing Control."
Being vulnerable doesn't require you to tell everyone anything about yourself. It's about deliberately opting to express yourself in ways that are authentic to you.

3."Strong People Don't Need Help."
Knowing when to ask for help is a sign of strength. Opening out to people or asking for assistance is not a sign of weakness but rather of self-awareness and perseverance.

One of the most potent ways to love oneself is to be vulnerable. It enables you to embrace the whole range of your human experience, respect your feelings, and form meaningful connections with other people. You'll learn that being vulnerable is not a weakness but rather a powerful quality

that influences your relationships, inner life, and creativity.
Redefining vulnerability as courage allows you to claim your true power and demonstrates that being vulnerable and open is not only courageous but also transformative.

Chapter 9

Choosing the Right Darkness

Not all types of sadness are the same. This chapter explores the distinction between destructive despair and creative sadness.

Not all types of sadness are the same. Some types of sadness present a chance for development, introspection, and creativity, while others can feel stifling and destructive. This chapter explores the complex range of melancholy and how to identify and interact with its different manifestations. We may develop a better relationship with our emotions and learn to move forward with clarity and purpose by learning to distinguish between destructive despair and creative grief.

One encourages reflection and personal development, while the other may result in destructive patterns. Here, we go over how to recognise and move through different phases, choose routes that replenish rather than exhaust.

Tools for self-evaluation, establishing sound emotional boundaries, and asking for assistance when necessary are introduced in this chapter. Not all darkness is bad. While some shadows consume, others provide cover.

The Two Faces of Sadness

1. Destructive Despair: The Consuming Shadow
Destructive despair is a weighty, lonely, and never-ending feeling. It frequently results in negative rumination, depressing thoughts, and actions that feed the vicious cycle of suffering. You may become weary, disengaged, and stuck in this kind of grief.

Characteristics:
1. Persistent negative thoughts that spiral.
2. A sense of being trapped or overwhelmed.
3. Avoidance of meaningful connections or activities.

2. Creative Sadness: The Reflective Shadow
In contrast, creative sadness encourages reflection and change. Even while it's still difficult, it can lead to inspiration, insight, and personal development. This kind of melancholy inspires you to find purpose in challenging situations and process feelings in a healthy way.

Characteristics:

1. Encourages reflection and self-awareness.
2. Leads to problem-solving or emotional breakthroughs.
3. Inspires creativity or fosters empathy for others.

Navigating the Spectrum of Sadness

1. Emotional Self-Assessment

The first step is figuring out where you are on the sadness continuum. Being self-aware enables you to recognise whether your melancholy is pushing you in the direction of progress or dragging you into despair.

How to Practice Emotional Self-Assessment:

Daily Check-In:
Write down how you feel at the end of each day.
Reflection Scale:
Rate your sadness on a scale:
1-3: Constructive sadness (helpful reflection, insight).
4-6: Neutral sadness (neither constructive nor destructive).
7-10: Destructive despair (harmful rumination, overwhelming pain).

Patterns Over Time:

Look for trends. Are there triggers or circumstances that push your sadness into a destructive zone?

You can obtain clarity and take action before harmful patterns take hold by routinely evaluating your feelings.

2. Establishing Emotional Boundaries

Sadness can take up your thoughts and energy if you don't set boundaries. You can analyse your feelings without becoming overwhelmed by them if you place boundaries on how you interact with them.

Practical Boundary Techniques:

Time-Limited Reflection:
Set a timer for 20 minutes. During this time, allow yourself to feel and explore your sadness—write, cry, or sit with your thoughts. When the timer rings, shift gears to a grounding exercise or activity that brings you back to the present.
Emotion-Free Zones:
Dedicate specific times or spaces (e.g., meals, shared activities) where you consciously step away from ruminating.
Compartmentalization Practice:
Visualize placing your sadness in a mental "container." Tell yourself you'll revisit it later but, for now, focus on something restorative.

Setting limits gives you a sense of control and keeps your melancholy from permeating every area of your life.

3. Seeking Support When Needed

Sadness can be too much to bear on one's own at times. One of the most important skills for reducing isolation and increasing resilience is knowing when to reach out.

Steps to Seek Support:

Identify Trusted Allies:
Make a list of people you can turn to, such as friends, family, therapists, or support groups.
Be Specific About Your Needs:
Instead of saying, "I feel sad," try, "I'm feeling overwhelmed and could use someone to talk to."
Professional Help:
If sadness persists or intensifies, consult a therapist or counselor who can provide tools and guidance tailored to your experience.
Peer Support Groups:
Joining a community where others share similar experiences can be deeply validating and comforting.

Making connections with people, whether through personal or professional interactions, helps you see things from new angles and reminds you that you're not alone.

Harnessing the Power of Creative Sadness

1. Turning Reflection into Action
Examine your life through the prism of your grief. Are there unresolved feelings or unfulfilled needs that need to be addressed? Allow your melancholy to lead you to significant transformation.

Ideas for Constructive Reflection:

1. Write about what your sadness is trying to tell you.
2. Identify one small step to address the root of your feelings .

2. Fostering Creativity and Empathy

Some of the best pieces of literature, music, and art have been influenced by sadness. Write a poem, paint a picture, or work on a personal project to express your feelings.

Creative Exercises:

1. Paint or draw your emotions as abstract shapes or colors.
2. Write a letter to your sadness, asking it what it wants from you.
3. Compose a piece of music or playlist that captures your mood.

3. Finding Meaning in Struggles

Reframe your unhappiness as a chance for personal development. What do you think I can learn about myself from this? How can it make me stronger or more sympathetic?

Finding Balance in Shadows

Darkness is not always the same. Some shadows offer protection where development and change can take place, while others consume. You can manage your emotions more easily and purposefully if you can tell the difference between creative grief and destructive despair.

You don't have to let sadness define you; it may be a tool for creativity, self-discovery, and connection. Sadness can be viewed as a teacher that leads to increased understanding and resilience when it is addressed with care and curiosity.

Chapter 10

Living the Paradox

Accepting depression while still striving for joy is the paradox of the happiest depressed life. Frustration and optimism, joy and sadness, loss and thankfulness—these are all strands in the intricate fabric of human experience, not opposing states of existence. The challenge of leading a "happy depressed life" is to learn to live with contradictions and flourish in the midst of life's inconsistencies, not to eradicate suffering or discover a conclusive solution to internal conflicts.

In order to assist readers in navigating the highs and lows of their path with grace and sincerity, this chapter explores the art of embracing dualities and provides resources and insights.

The Art of Paradox

1. The Paradox of Coexistence

Darkness and light may coexist, despite the fact that depression frequently forces us to choose between the two. Joy is not invalidated by pain, and happy moments do not erase sadness. This coexistence is fundamental to what it means to be human, not a weakness in our emotional constitution.

We can liberate ourselves from the tiresome quest of "fixing" our grief or guilt about finding joy in the midst of suffering by accepting this paradox. Rather, we learn to make room for both feelings, letting them influence and improve our lives.

2. The Happiness-Sadness Spectrum

Emotions belong to a spectrum rather than being binary. On certain days, you might be more inclined to one side than the other, and on other days, you might be in the precarious middle ground where happiness and sorrow coexist. You can approach your emotional condition with curiosity rather than condemnation if you understand its mobility.

Tools for Embracing Contradictions

1. Dual Journaling

By keeping a dual journal, you can investigate how seemingly incompatible feelings can coexist.

How to Practice:

1.Divide your journal page into two columns. Label one side Grief or Darkness and the other

Moments of Light.

2.On the Grief side, write about the struggles, pain, or moments of despair you've faced that day.

3.On the Moments of Light side, reflect on small joys or glimmers of hope you encountered—a kind gesture, a favorite song, a beautiful sunset.

You can visually recognise the harmony of light and dark in your life with the help of this practice. It reaffirms that happiness and sadness can coexist without negating one another.

2. Acceptance Practices

Resignation is not acceptance. Rather, it is a strong act of self-compassion that makes room for recovery and development.

Mantra for Acceptance:
Find a quiet place to sit, close your eyes, and breathe deeply. As you exhale, repeat the mantra: **"I can be both happy and sad. Both are true. Both are valid."**

Variations to Explore:
1.Place your hand on your chest as you recite the mantra to ground yourself in the moment.

2.Use this practice when you feel conflicted about experiencing joy during a difficult time.

You can embrace the completeness of your emotional reality and let go of the temptation to "fix" yourself by engaging in acceptance techniques.

3. Stories of Paradox

Many people have lived and prospered throughout history in the dichotomy of extreme joy and misery. We can be motivated to accept contrasts in our own lives by their stories.

Examples of Paradoxical Lives:

Vincent van Gogh:
Struggled with mental illness but created art that continues to inspire awe and wonder.

Maya Angelou:
Overcame immense personal hardship and became a beacon of resilience and hope through her words.

Winston Churchill:
Battled depressive episodes (his "black dog") while leading a nation through its darkest times.

How to Engage with These Stories:

Read articles, autobiographies, or biographies that explore the lives of those who succeeded in spite of or as a result of their hardships.

Consider how their legacy was shaped by their capacity to hold conflicting truths.

Managing Contradictions in Daily Life

1. Practical Mindset Shifts
It takes a change in viewpoint to live a life of contradictions:

Reframe "Confusion" as Growth:
Feeling torn between emotions isn't a sign of failure but of emotional complexity and depth.
Recognize the Wholeness in Inconsistencies:
You don't have to choose between being "happy" or "sad." You are already whole, contradictions and all.

2. Creative Expression of Dualities

Art is a powerful way to explore and express paradoxes.

Visual Arts:
Create a painting or collage that juxtaposes light and dark, joy and sorrow.
Writing Prompts:
Write a poem or short story that captures the duality of emotions you've felt in a single moment.

Eradicating melancholy or creating joy is not the goal of the paradox of leading a happy depressed existence. It is about recognising the depth of the human experience, finding harmony in conflict, and learning to dance with the darkness.

You can embrace a life that is beautifully, messily, truly both by including techniques like dual journaling, acceptance techniques, and the study of paradoxical lives. This will help you get over the binary attitude of "broken or whole," "happy or sad."

The goal of this journey is to learn to live fully amid contradictions rather than to resolve them; this lesson has the power to change not just how you view depression but also how you view yourself.

Chapter 11

The Lies We Tell Ourselves

Self-deception can catch even the most self-aware people. We create stories to protect ourselves from suffering, to defend our alleged flaws, or to avoid the awkwardness of facing harsh realities. When you're far from okay, these lies frequently murmur hurtful messages like "I'm not enough" or "I'm fine." Although these tales may provide momentary comfort, they frequently exacerbate wounds over time, trapping us in cycles of avoidance and self-doubt.

Through gentle truth-telling—an method that emphasises honesty tempered with compassion—rather than harsh self-criticism, this chapter asks you to expose these self-deceptions. You can start rewriting these damaging narratives into ones of empowerment and self-acceptance by addressing them in a compassionate and encouraging manner.

Why Do We Lie to Ourselves?

1. Self-Protection:
We frequently tell lies to spare ourselves the agony of confronting harsh truths. Saying things like "I'm fine" or "It's not a big deal" can act as a buffer from the crushing reality.

2. Fear of Vulnerability:
Admitting our difficulties could make us feel vulnerable or helpless. Projecting strength—even if it's a façade—is simpler than running the risk of appearing vulnerable.

3. Avoiding Accountability:
Self-deception can occasionally result from a refusal to face the work necessary for change. Saying, "This is just how I am," releases us from accountability.

4. Internalized Criticism:
External judgements have the potential to be internalised over time. Instead of being based on objective facts, statements like "I'm not good enough" or "I'll never get better" are frequently the result of familial or societal pressures.

Common Lies We Tell Ourselves

1. "I'm fine."
This delusion minimises your difficulties, which frequently results in emotional exhaustion.

2. "I'm not enough."
The plot diminishes confidence and feeds feelings of inadequacy since it is rooted in self-doubt.

3. "No one cares."
Depression can isolate you, making it easy to believe that others are indifferent to your pain.

4. "It's my fault."
A tendency to blame yourself for circumstances beyond your control reinforces guilt and shame.

5. "I don't deserve happiness."
This delusion deepens sadness by sustaining the idea that happiness is unachievable or undeserving.

The Practice of Gentle Truth-Telling

1. Awareness Without Judgment
The first step in confronting self-deception is recognizing it. Journaling can be a helpful tool:

(a) Write down the negative thoughts or beliefs that frequently arise.
(b) Ask yourself: "Is this thought based on fact or feeling?"

for Example:

Lie: "I'm not enough."

Truth: "I feel like I'm not enough because I'm comparing myself to unrealistic standards. But my worth isn't defined by these measures."

2. Reframing Negative Narratives

Once a negative thought has been found, gently reframe it into a more positive truth. Finding a balanced viewpoint is more important than being overly optimistic.

Example:

Lie: "No one cares about me."

Reframe: "It feels like no one cares because I've been isolating myself. But I know people who have shown care before, and I can reach out to them."

3. Compassionate Self-Talk

Kind, encouraging, and affirming language should take the place of critical inner conversation.

Asking yourself, "What would I say to a friend in this situation?" can help you identify self-critical thoughts. Say those things to yourself after that.

Example:

Lie: "It's my fault that things went wrong."

Truth: "I did my best with what I knew at the time. Mistakes are part of being human."

Tools for Practicing Gentle Truth-Telling

1. Truth Journaling:
Write down any lies you catch yourself believing in a special section of your journal. Provide a kind truth in response to each one.

Example :
Lie: "I don't deserve happiness."

Truth: "I am worthy of happiness, even if I'm struggling. Joy and pain can coexist, and I don't need to be perfect to deserve good things."

2. Daily Affirmations:

Write or speak affirmations that challenge your self-deceptions. Examples include:

"I am enough, just as I am."
"I deserve love and care, even on my hardest days."
"My struggles do not define my worth."

3. Dialogue with Your Inner Critic:

Consider your self-deceptive beliefs to be the result of an inner voice that is well-intentioned yet incorrect. Take a caring approach to it:

"I hear you saying I'm not enough, but I know you're trying to protect me from disappointment. I am enough, even when things are hard."

When to Seek Support

Although speaking the truth gently can be a powerful technique, certain lies are deeply rooted and may need to be separated with expert assistance. See a therapist or counsellor if you're having trouble dealing with damaging narratives on your own. In a secure and encouraging setting, they can assist you in understanding and disputing these ideas.

Although self-deception frequently stems from suffering, it should not define you. Gentle truth-telling allows you to challenge damaging narratives without demeaning yourself. With this method, you can establish a relationship with yourself that is based on compassion and honesty, which serves as a basis for recovery and development.

Unmasking lies is about releasing yourself from their burden and entering a place of greater self-awareness and acceptance, not about punishing yourself for believing them. Adopting this approach allows you to reclaim your story as one of bravery, resiliency, and authenticity rather than one of brokenness.

Chapter 12

Redefining Success

When happiness isn't the ultimate goal, what does success look like? In a society where success is defined by significant achievements and unwavering happiness, it's simple to feel left behind if joy is difficult to find. This chapter questions accepted notions of success and advises readers to emphasise resilience, personal fulfilment, and the small wins that add significance to life—especially in trying times.

Awards and mountain climbing are not necessary for success. Finding a moment of calm in the midst of the commotion, getting out of bed, or finishing a meal are all examples of how to show up for yourself. Redefining success celebrates the bravery required to persevere when it seems like the odds are stacked against you and moves the focus from results to effort.

Why Redefine Success?

1. The Burden of Traditional Success
Success is frequently equated with financial wealth, production, and public acknowledgement by societal norms. These standards may seem unachievable to someone who is depressed, which could result in feelings of failure or inadequacy.

2. The Need for Personal Milestones
The very personal and frequently undetectable victories that signify progress for someone dealing with mental health issues are not taken into consideration by traditional success metrics.

3.The Power of Small Wins
Little accomplishments like getting dressed, answering a friend's message, or making something worthwhile are worthy of praise. They remind us that there is no one-size-fits-all approach to achievement.

What Does Success Look Like When It's Not About Happiness?

1.Effort Over Outcome:
Success is not just about where you end up, but also about the actions you take. Even in its flaws, trying to take care of yourself is something to be proud of.

2.Presence Over Perfection:

Being present on your journey and gracefully appreciating both successes and losses is more important than having it all together.

3.Fulfillment Over Metrics:

What feeds you is what truly succeeds, whether it's a creative endeavour, a deep connection, or just getting through a difficult day.

Practices for Redefining Success

1. Set Unconventional Goals

Setting traditional goals can be intimidating, particularly if they are dependent on approval from others. Rather, concentrate on modest, doable objectives that respect your present abilities.

Examples:
"Today, I will spend 5 minutes in the sunlight."
"I will write one sentence in my journal".
"I will drink a glass of water first thing in the morning."

Although these objectives may not appear important to others, they represent critical turning points in your journey towards resilience and care.

2. Track Your "Wins" in a Journal

Establish a place where daily successes, no matter how minor, can be documented. By doing this, the focus changes from self-criticism to self-appreciation.

Examples of Wins to Celebrate:
Getting out of bed when it felt impossible.
Having a conversation when isolation seemed easier.
Finding beauty in a fleeting moment, like a bird's song or the warmth of a cup of tea.

suggestion :
Revisit this journal on harder days to remind yourself of your strength.

3. Celebrate Progress Over Perfection

Perfection is an illusion, but progress is real and worthy of celebration. Find ways to mark milestones that feel authentic to you.

Reward yourself with something simple, like a favorite snack or a comforting activity, when you complete a challenging task.

Reflect on how far you've come, even if it feels incremental. Progress isn't linear, and every step counts.

Exercises for Redefining Success

1. Daily Effort Tracker:
Instead of listing tasks to accomplish, create a tracker for efforts made. For example:

Took a deep breath when feeling overwhelmed.
Responded to one email.
Practiced kindness towards yourself.

Recognize that effort, not outcome, is where success lies.

2. Joy and Resilience Inventory:

Create a list of moments where you felt resilient or found unexpected joy. This might include:

Laughing at something absurd.
Finding a spark of creativity.
Choosing to keep going despite the weight of the day.

3. The "Good Enough" List:

Write down things you've done that might not feel extraordinary but were "good enough" for the day.

Examples:
Cooked a simple meal instead of skipping it.
Rested instead of forcing productivity.
Reached out to a friend.

Stories of Success in Small Victories

In order to provide motivation, this section presents stories of people who achieved success in the most unlikely places:

The Artist Who Painted Through the Darkness:

Despite crippling self-doubt, they created one small piece of art each day, finding solace in the act of creating, not the outcome.

The Parent Who Chose to Pause:

On a hard day, instead of pushing through exhaustion, they chose to rest and reconnect with their children, redefining success as presence rather than performance.

There is no one universal definition of success. Its definitions change over time and depending on the situation, and it is quite personal. Success can entail surviving, persevering, or finding moments of light in the dark when happiness isn't the ultimate aim.

By accepting non-traditional standards of accomplishment, you give yourself permission to live really and respect your path, no matter how convoluted or sluggish it may seem. Every tiny triumph demonstrates your tenacity and serves as a subdued yet potent reminder that putting yourself first, no matter how flawed, is an accomplishment to be proud of.

Chapter 13

Finding Meaning in the Struggle

"Suffering ceases to be suffering at the moment it finds meaning," as said by Viktor Frankl, is a hopeful statement, but it also poses a difficult query: How do we discover meaning when life seems unmanageable? This chapter explores the quest for meaning in the face of adversity, not as a definitive solution but as a very personal experience. Meaning is frequently found in little, peaceful moments or a basic sense of connection rather than in big breakthroughs.

Why Seek Meaning?

1.The Role of Meaning in Endurance:
Meaning serves as a stabilising force, giving pain context and motivation to endure. It changes pain into something more tolerable, even transformative, but it doesn't completely eradicate it.

2.Meaning Is Personal, Not Prescriptive:
Meaning is different for each person than what society considers to be success or happiness. It doesn't have to involve great accomplishments; it could just be about being there for the people or things that are important to you.

3.The Power of Purpose in Struggle:
Chaos is given shape by purpose, which serves as a reminder that even in the most hopeless circumstances, there is something worthwhile to hold on to, such as a relationship, a creative effort, or just the will to live.

Ways to Discover Meaning

1. Relationships as a Source of Meaning
We are often grounded by connection when life seems too much to handle. Meaning doesn't have to be elaborate; it can be as easy as sharing a sensitive moment, supporting a friend, or being there for a loved one.

Exercise:
Reflect on one relationship that brings you a sense of purpose. Write down a moment when this relationship provided strength or comfort.

2. Creativity as Expression

Many people find that being creative is a lifeline, a means of processing feelings, and a means of connecting with something more than themselves. Writing, painting, singing, or even keeping a journal is an example of making art for its own sake, not for the benefit of others.

Exercise:
Dedicate 10 minutes daily to a creative outlet. It doesn't have to be perfect; the act itself is meaningful.

3. Presence in the Small Things
The mundane-the way sunlight filters through leaves, the sound of laughing, or the act of doing a task-often conceals meaning. You make room to see and value these moments when you slow down.

Exercise:
At the end of each day, write down one small, meaningful moment you noticed.

Tools for Discovering Meaning

1. Write a Personal Manifesto
A manifesto is a statement of your beliefs, goals, and tenets. It's a means of expressing your priorities and can act as a compass during trying times.

Steps to Create a Manifesto:
Start with this question: What do I care about most deeply?
Write freely for 10 minutes, letting your thoughts flow.
Distill your thoughts into 3-5 guiding principles.

Example:
I value connection with others, even in small ways.
I commit to finding beauty in imperfection.
I honor my resilience by continuing to try.

2. Identify Your Core Values

In times of uncertainty, values serve as a north star, offering direction and clarity. When life seems chaotic, thinking back on them might help you stay grounded.

Exercise to Identify Core Values:
Make a list of words that resonate with you, such as "kindness," "creativity," "community," or "resilience."
Choose 3-5 that feel most authentic.
Reflect on how these values show up in your life or how you can honor them.

3. The Power of Legacy

Think about the influence you wish to leave—not in a big way, but in the way you affect other people's lives. This could entail being known for your bravery, friendliness, or readiness to show up even in the face of difficulty.

Exercise:
Write a letter to yourself or someone you care about, expressing the legacy you hope to create.

Finding Meaning Through Stories

1.Personal Narratives:

Stories of others who found meaning in struggle can inspire and remind us that we're not alone.
For example:
A mother finding purpose in advocating for mental health after her child's challenges.

An artist turning their grief into a body of work that resonates with others.

2.Your Own Story:
Even if your path is disorganised or unfinished, it still has purpose. You can be reminded of your strength by taking stock of your progress and the tenacity you've displayed.

Exercises to Anchor Meaning

1. Gratitude Letters:
Compose a letter to something or someone that has given your life purpose. This might be a favourite spot, a pet, or even a friend.

2. Purpose Mapping:
Make a visual map of your meaning-giving activities. Create a central circle called "Meaning" and then add branches representing the relationships, pursuits, or ideals that are important to you.

3. Mantras for Meaning:
Create a short mantra to remind yourself of your purpose.
Examples:
"I am here for connection."
"Each moment holds value."
"I am enough as I am."

In times of extreme stress, finding meaning involves integrating suffering into a larger fabric of connection and purpose rather than trying to erase it. Through connections, creativity, or just deciding to keep going, meaning provides a means of overcoming obstacles in life with grace and resiliency.
This search does not have to lead to a single discovery or be linear. Meaning can be found in both short-lived events and long-term commitments. Seeking meaning is a silent but powerful method to confirm your position in the world, and it is a testimonial to your strength in and of itself.

Chapter 14

The Quiet Power of Rituals

Fundamentally, rituals are deliberate actions that give our lives direction and significance. They provide us with stability even in the midst of a turbulent environment by keeping us rooted in the here and now. Rituals don't have to be elaborate or ceremonial; they can be modest, straightforward actions that provide solace and a feeling of authority.

This chapter examines the ways in which rituals can act as anchor points during emotionally charged periods, promoting mental calmness, spiritual development, and a feeling of direction.

Why Rituals Matter

1.A Sense of Control:
Rituals serve as a reminder of our controllable aspects in the midst of chaos. These routines, whether you follow them in the morning or at the end of the evening, provide predictable and secure moments.

2.Emotional Grounding:
Rituals give us emotional stability and a respite from the chaos of everyday life. By providing a place to think or just be, they enable us to re-establish a connection with ourselves.

3.Symbolism and Meaning:
Intentionally repeating even little actions gives them more meaning. A evening walk turns into a place to let go of the stresses of the day, and a morning cup of coffee becomes an opportunity to express thanks.

Types of Rituals

1. Daily Anchors
These are rituals tied to specific times of the day that help create a sense of rhythm and flow.

Examples:

Morning Rituals:

Brew your coffee or tea mindfully, focusing on the aroma, warmth, and taste.
Spend five minutes journaling your intentions for the day.

Evening Rituals:

Light a candle to signify the transition to rest.
Write down one thing you're grateful for before bed.

2. Mindful Movement

Physical activity-based rituals can facilitate mental-physical communication, allowing pent-up energy to be released and fostering a sense of peace.

Examples:

A daily walk at the same time each day, focusing on the sights and sounds around you.
Stretching or yoga to mark the start or end of your day.

3. Creative Rituals

Emotions can be effectively released through creativity, and ritualising artistic endeavours can strengthen this bond.

Examples:
Sketching or painting for a few minutes each day, even if it's abstract.
Writing a single poem, line, or thought to capture your mood.

4. Connection Rituals

Rituals that foster connection with others or nature can be deeply fulfilling and grounding.

Examples:
Sharing a meal with a loved one without distractions.
Spending time in nature, such as watering plants or watching the sunrise.

How to Create Your Own Rituals

1. Identify Your Needs:
Think about what you need most in your life at the moment: structure, inspiration, connection, or serenity. These needs should be met by your rituals.

Questions to Consider:
What moments of my day feel most overwhelming or empty?
Where can I carve out time for intentionality?
What simple actions bring me comfort or joy?

2. Start Small:

Rituals don't have to be laborious or complex. Build from a manageable starting point, such as a 5-minute exercise.

3. Infuse Intention:
Intention distinguishes a ritual from a routine. Treat your acts as precious moments rather than as tasks and approach them mindfully.

4. Make It Personal:
Adapt your rituals to your emotional requirements and preferences. While preparing bread or setting up a space could be rituals for one individual, meditation might be for another.

5. Create a Ritual Space:
Set aside a place, either mental or physical, for your routines. It might be a comfortable chair for writing in a diary, a peaceful nook for meditation, or just a clear head when you go outside.

Enhancing the Ritual Experience

Use Symbols:
Incorporate objects like candles, crystals, or specific tools to imbue your ritual with meaning.
Combine Senses:
Engage multiple senses—sight, sound, touch, smell, and taste—to make your rituals more immersive.
For example, light a scented candle while listening to calming music during your evening routine.
Track Your Rituals:
Use a journal or app to track your rituals, reflecting on how they impact your mood and well-being over time.

Examples of Healing Rituals

1. The Morning Reset
Start the day with a deep breath.
Write down one intention or affirmation.
Sip your coffee or tea while looking out a window or listening to calming music.

2. The Evening Release
Light a candle to signify the end of the day.
Write a short reflection on something you learned or experienced.
Stretch or practice slow, intentional movements to release tension.

3. Nature Connection
Spend five minutes outside, barefoot if possible, focusing on the sensation of the ground beneath you.
Collect small natural objects like leaves or stones to create a "nature altar" as a reminder of your connection to the world.

4. Creativity Corner
Set aside time for a creative ritual, such as journaling, drawing, or playing music.

Dedicate this time solely to exploration without judgment or goals.

Rituals give life's uncertainties a consistent beat, keeping us rooted in the here and now while providing opportunities for introspection, comfort, and purpose. We create opportunities to connect with ourselves, control our emotions, and find stability in the midst of chaos by incorporating tiny, deliberate activities into our everyday life.

Rituals ultimately serve as a reminder that there is meaning and strength in even the simplest deeds. We regain control over our days and start to heal via these holy moments—not by removing the turmoil, but by bringing peace to it.

Chapter 15

Learning to Say No (and Yes)

Our sense of agency can be distorted by depression, making it difficult to distinguish between what we need, what we want, and what we can manage. Because of fear, fatigue, or self-doubt, we may end up accepting things that drain us or turning down possibilities. Regaining your ability to make decisions is the focus of this chapter. You will learn how to establish limits that safeguard your energy while keeping your mind open to opportunities for growth, joy, and connection.

The Dual Struggle: Saying No and Saying Yes

1.Saying No with Confidence:
Depression frequently results in an increased sense of duty or guilt, which makes it difficult to say no, even when a circumstance puts your mental well-being in jeopardy. Setting limits is a necessary part of self-preservation, not selfishness.

2.Saying Yes with Courage:
Conversely, depression can also result in avoidance and loneliness, which makes it hard to say yes to opportunities that could support or encourage you. One of the most important aspects of recovery is learning to know when to risk joy or connection.

Why Boundaries Matter

Energy Preservation:
Boundaries help conserve your limited emotional and physical energy, ensuring that you have enough for the things that truly matter.

Clarity of Purpose:
Saying no to what drains you creates space for activities and relationships that align with your values and needs.

Emotional Safety:
Boundaries protect you from situations that exacerbate your depression, whether it's toxic relationships, overcommitment, or unhealthy environments.

Tools for Setting Boundaries

1. Assess Your Emotional Bandwidth
Take a moment each day to reflect on your current capacity.

Ask yourself:
How much energy do I have to give today?
What tasks or interactions feel manageable versus overwhelming?

Exercise:
List the interactions or activities you expect to have during the day and classify them as draining, neutral, or energy-giving to create a "emotional budget." Adapt your obligations in light of this budget.

2. Practice Assertive Communication

Setting boundaries doesn't require elaborate explanations.
Practice simple, clear statements such as:

"I can't commit to that right now."
"I need some time to think before I decide."
"Thank you for understanding, but I have to say no."

3. Set Non-Negotiables

Identify key areas where you need firm boundaries to protect your well-being.

These might include:
Allocating time for rest without interruptions.
Limiting contact with individuals who trigger or drain you.
Protecting your self-care routines, such as therapy or exercise.

Saying Yes: Embracing Moments of Growth

Boundaries are important, but so is being open to chances that challenge the inertia of despair, joy, and connection.

1. Recognize the Fear Behind No
Sometimes, saying no isn't about protecting your energy but about avoiding vulnerability or risk.

Ask yourself:
Am I saying no out of fear of failure or rejection?
Could this opportunity contribute to my growth or happiness, even in small ways?

2. Start with Low-Stakes Yeses

Saying yes doesn't have to mean committing to grand gestures. Begin with small, manageable steps, such as:
Agreeing to meet a friend for a short coffee date.
Trying a creative hobby for 10 minutes.
Taking a short walk in a new place.

3. Reflect on Past Wins

Think back to times when answering "yes," despite the initial difficulty, resulted in something good. Gain confidence in your capacity to take chances by using these experiences.

Exercises for Reclaiming Choice

1. The Boundary Audit

List areas of your life where you struggle to say no.
Reflect on the consequences of not setting boundaries in those areas.
Write one clear boundary you want to implement and how you'll communicate it.

2. The Yes Journal

Each day, write down one small thing you said yes to, even if it was daunting.
Reflect on how it felt and any positive outcomes that came from it.

3. Permission Slips

Write yourself a "permission slip" for the day, such as:
"I give myself permission to say no to anything that feels draining."
"I give myself permission to say yes to a moment of joy or connection."

The Balancing Act

Finding balance is more important than firmly declaring yes or no if you want to regain the power of choice. Setting boundaries makes room for deliberate choices, but being open prevents you from losing sight of the beauties and possibilities of life.

It takes time to learn how to strike this equilibrium. On some days, you'll take chances and embrace the unexpected, but on others, you'll zealously guard your energy. Even when dealing with the difficulties of depression, this intentionality practice can eventually provide you a greater sense of control over your life.

You regain your agency—and with it, the ability to direct your life as you see fit—by taking back your freedom of choice.

Chapter 16

The Healing Power of Creativity

Depression frequently resembles a fog that obscures our perceptions and numbs our feelings. However, creativity provides a path through that haze—not by clearing everything away, but by transforming it into something concrete, significant, and exclusively yours. This chapter examines how finding artistic outlets can help turn suffering into a source of meaning and beauty, providing catharsis, clarity, and a fresh sense of self.

The Process, Not the Product

The idea that creativity is all about the result—a completed artwork, a best-selling book, or the ideal dish—is among the worst fallacies about it. In actuality, the act of creating, not the final product, is what gives creativity its strength. This technique can be quite therapeutic for people who are depressed:

Emotional Release:
Putting feelings into words, colors, or actions provides a safe outlet for emotions that may feel overwhelming or difficult to articulate.
Presence in the Moment:
Creating demands attention and focus, pulling you into the present moment and away from intrusive thoughts.
Rediscovery of Joy:
The act of creating, even something as simple as doodling or arranging flowers, can spark small moments of joy and accomplishment.

Choosing Your Creative Outlet

Since creativity is so individualised, there is no one-size-fits-all method. Finding a hobby that appeals to you is crucial, regardless of whether you're drawn to writing, music, visual arts, or something else completely.

1. Visual Arts

Painting or Drawing:
Use colors and shapes to express emotions you can't put into words.
Collage Making: Cut out images, words, or textures from magazines to create a mood board

that represents your feelings.

Photography:
Capture small moments of beauty around you—shadows, textures, or colors that catch your eye.

2. Writing

Journaling:
Write freely about your emotions, thoughts, or memories without worrying about grammar or structure.

Poetry:
Use metaphor and rhythm to explore your feelings in a creative way.

Fiction:
Create characters or stories that help you process your own experiences from a distance.

3. Crafts and Hobbies

Knitting or Crochet:
The repetitive motions can be meditative, and the act of creating something tangible is deeply rewarding.

Gardening:
Connecting with nature by planting, tending, and harvesting can bring a sense of nurturing and growth.

Cooking or Baking:
Experiment with new recipes or recreate comforting dishes from your past.

4. Music and Movement

Playing an Instrument:
Even simple melodies can help express emotions.

Singing:
Letting your voice carry your feelings can be liberating.

Dancing:
Move your body freely to music, focusing on the sensations rather than the steps.

Creativity as Catharsis

Creativity has the power to help you process and release emotions in a way that words alone cannot.

For instance:

Art as a Mirror:
When you paint or write, you often uncover feelings or patterns you weren't consciously aware of.

Art as a Container:
By putting your emotions into something external—a canvas, a poem, or a sculpture—you give yourself permission to step back and view them from a safer distance.

Art as Transformation:

Turning pain into art transforms it into something meaningful, something you've actively shaped rather than something that controls you.

Practical Exercises

1. Mood Mapping with Colors
Make a map of your feelings using shades. For happiness, use warm tones; for peace use cool tones; for sadness, use dark shades; and for wrath, use strong shades. Make decisions based on your intuition.

2. Word Dump Journaling
Set a timer for 10 minutes and write whatever comes to mind without stopping. Don't worry about coherence—this exercise is about letting your thoughts flow freely.

3. Sensory Collage
To create a tactile depiction of your feelings, collect sensory-rich things such as pictures, dried flowers, textured paper, and soft fabrics, and place them on a board.

4. Daily Doodles
Whether it's a fast sketch of something you observe or an abstract design, make it a daily goal to doodle in your little sketchbook.

5. Song of the Day
Pick a song that matches your mood and either sing along, move to it, or simply let it wash over you.

Overcoming Creative Blocks

Feeling uninspired or trapped is normal, especially when you're depressed.
Here's how to navigate those blocks gently:

Lower the Stakes:
Remind yourself that what you create doesn't have to be "good" or even finished. It's about the process, not perfection.
Start Small:
Begin with a 5-minute creative activity. Often, starting is the hardest part.
Seek Inspiration:
Look at art, read poetry, or listen to music that resonates with you. Let others' creativity spark your own.
Be Kind to Yourself:
If a creative activity feels like too much, that's okay. Give yourself permission to rest and try again later.

While it doesn't guarantee a cure for depression, creativity provides a means of overcoming it.

It might serve as a reminder that you are capable of doing something significant even in the most difficult circumstances. You can reconnect with the more profound, enduring aspects of yourself and regain your sense of agency by turning your suffering into art.

By incorporating tiny creative endeavours into your life, you demonstrate that there is always room for expression and hope, even in the face of adversity.

Chapter 17

The Role of Gratitude in the Darkness

When despair consumes you, gratitude may seem unattainable. When just getting through the day feels like too much to handle, how can you be grateful? This chapter reinterprets gratitude as a gentle discipline of recognising glimmering rays of light in the dark, rather than as a rejection of suffering. Making space for brief but meaningful moments of comfort, beauty, or connection is more important than trying to force positive.

Gratitude Without Invalidating Pain

Gratitude is frequently misinterpreted as a call to "see the bright side" or to contrast your difficulties with those of others. This method may come across as harmful and contemptuous. Authentic thankfulness, on the other hand, makes room for appreciation while acknowledging your suffering. You can discover thankfulness in the experience of going through suffering, but you don't have to be thankful for the agony itself.

Dual Coexistence:

Gratitude and sadness can exist side by side. You can be thankful for a friend's support while still grieving your struggles.

Honoring Small Moments:

Gratitude doesn't have to be grandiose. It can be as simple as noticing the warmth of a cup of tea or the way sunlight filters through your window.

Permission to Feel Both:

It's okay to say, "Today was hard, but I'm thankful I made it through."

Cultivating Gratitude

Like a muscle, gratitude gets stronger with use.
Here are a few easy methods to get started:

1. The One-Line Journal

Write down one thing for which you are thankful at the end of each day. The statement "I had a moment of peace while listening to music" could be the simplest.

2. Gratitude Anchors

Find little "anchors" throughout your day that you can return to with gratitude, such as the sound of rain, the feel of a warm blanket, or the aroma of coffee brewing.

3. Kindness Reflection

Reflect on acts of kindness you've witnessed or received, no matter how small. Did someone hold the door open for you? Did a stranger smile at you?

4. Gratitude Walks

Go for a walk with the intention of noticing things to be grateful for.
Pay attention to the sights, sounds, and sensations that bring you even the smallest comfort.

5. Gratitude Letters

Write a letter (even if you don't send it) to someone who has impacted your life positively. This can be a cathartic way to connect with appreciation.

Balancing Gratitude and Authenticity

Being grateful does not mean denying your suffering or acting as though you are feeling better than you actually are. Rather, it's a way of making room for your challenges as well as the bright spots that accompany them.

1. Naming the Darkness and the Light

Acknowledge your pain openly before identifying something you're grateful for.
For example, you might say, "I felt really lonely today, but I'm grateful for the text my friend sent me."

2. The Gratitude Spectrum

Understand that there are several levels of gratitude. On certain days, you may feel grateful for significant things, such as the assistance of a loved one. On other days, it could simply be thankfulness for surviving the day. Both are legitimate.

3. Compassionate Gratitude

Be thankful for yourself. Even in difficult situations, give yourself credit for turning up. "Even though I only rested today, I'm glad I took care of myself."

Exercises to Begin

1. Five Senses Gratitude Practice

List one thing you're grateful for that you can see, hear, touch, taste, and smell. This brings your focus to the present moment and helps you notice small joys.

2. Gratitude Jar

Keep a jar and slips of paper nearby. Write down moments of gratitude as they happen. On tough days, revisit your collection of small blessings.

3. Morning or Evening Rituals

Start or end your day with a moment of gratitude. Reflect on what went right, no matter how small.

4. Gratitude Collage

Create a visual reminder of the things you're grateful for—photos, drawings, or mementos that symbolize moments of light in your life.

The Healing Power of Gratitude

Although it doesn't take away suffering, gratitude gives your experience more depth and character and enables you to recognise that both bright and evil can coexist. It's a silent recognition of the complexity of life and the fact that, even the most trying circumstances, there are still strands of beauty, connection, and hope to cling to.

By incorporating thankfulness into your life, you develop the practice of focussing on what keeps you going when everything else seems to be falling apart. By doing this, you recover a tiny but potent sense of agency—a reminder that grace can still exist even in the middle of sorrow.

Chapter 18

Rebuilding Connection

Depression has a way of making us think that the best course of action is to withdraw. It hints that you are a burden, that no one gets it, or that reaching out is too difficult. However, a link, no matter how tiny or basic, can serve as a lifeline, binding you to the world beyond your suffering.

This chapter highlights that restoring relationships during a depressive episode involves tiny, doable actions to restore communication, trust, and mutual understanding rather than large-scale gestures.

Why Connection Matters

Breaking Isolation's Cycle:
Isolation can deepen feelings of loneliness and despair. Connection helps remind you that you're not alone.

Shared Strength:
Relationships provide emotional support, encouragement, and perspective during difficult times.

Restoring Hope:
Even a single moment of shared laughter or understanding can be a powerful antidote to despair.

Communicating Your Needs

Communicating your wants and feelings to others is one of the difficulties associated with depression. Others may wish to assist but are unsure how, or they may see your quiet as a sign of indifference. Honest and transparent communication aids in closing these gaps.

1. Start Small

If talking feels overwhelming, try sending a text message or writing a short letter.

Begin with simple statements like:
"I'm having a hard time and could use some support."
"I miss you and want to reconnect, but I'm not sure where to start."

2. Be Honest but Gentle

Share what you're comfortable with.

For example:

"I've been feeling low lately, and it's hard for me to reach out, but I value our connection."
"Sometimes I just need someone to listen without trying to fix things."

3. Use a Metaphor

If expressing emotions feels difficult, describe your experience in relatable terms:

"It feels like I'm carrying a heavy backpack I can't put down. Sometimes I need help lightening the load."

Reconnecting with Loved Ones

It's not necessary to immediately engage in in-depth discussions in order to rebuild connections. Small, shared moments can sometimes lead to the most significant ties.

1. Low-Pressure Interactions

Suggest casual activities that don't require much energy, like:

Watching a movie together.
Going for a quiet walk.
Sharing a meal in comfortable silence.

2. Practice Active Listening

Relationships are reciprocal. While communicating your wants is vital, listening to others builds relationships and promotes understanding.

3. Apologize Without Shame

If depression has caused misunderstandings or distance, acknowledge it gently:
"I know I've been distant, and it's not because I don't care.
I've been struggling but want to reconnect."

Building New Connections

Looking for new connections might be a life-changing step if your current relationships are stressed or you don't have a support system.

1. Support Groups

Many communities offer in-person or online groups where people share experiences and encour-

agement.
These safe spaces can provide understanding without judgment.

2. Hobby-Based Communities

Join a class, club, or online group focused on something you enjoy, like art, gardening, or reading.
Shared interests make it easier to connect.

3. Volunteering

Helping others can create a sense of purpose and connection while introducing you to people with similar values.

Setting Boundaries in Relationships

Reconnecting is vital, but so is safeguarding your emotional reserves. It's acceptable to establish limits in order to prevent overstretching oneself, as depression can make you feel vulnerable.

1. Be Clear About Your Limits

Communicate what you can and cannot handle:
"I'd love to talk, but I might not have the energy for a long conversation."

2. Say No Without Guilt

Declining an invitation doesn't mean you're rejecting the person.
Frame it kindly:
"I appreciate the invite, but I need to rest today. Can we reschedule?"

3. Avoid Toxic Dynamics

Pay attention to relationships that drain or harm you.
Prioritize connections that feel safe, supportive, and affirming.

Practical Exercises

1. Letter to a Friend

Write a letter (even if you don't send it) to someone you miss. Share memories, express gratitude, or update them on your life.

2. The One-Sentence Check-In

Commit to sending one brief message a day to someone you care about.
For example:

"Thinking of you—hope your day is going well."

3. Connection Journal

Track small moments of connection each day, whether it's a smile from a stranger, a kind word, or a brief chat with a loved one.

4. Connection Goals

Set manageable goals, like calling one friend a week or attending one social activity per month. Celebrate each step forward.

Embracing the Power of Connection

Perseverance is more important than perfection when it comes to repairing and preserving connections during depression. Little gestures of kindness serve as a reminder that you are important and that you are a part of something bigger.

Reaching out, no matter how uncomfortable or unfinished it may feel, is an act of courage, even when depression pushes you to withdraw. By taking these tiny actions, you mend relationships with people and find solace and strength in our common humanity.

Chapter 19

Making Peace with Time

Depression can change how we see time, compressing weeks into a blurred blur or making moments seem to last forever. Feelings of alienation are frequently exacerbated by this warping of time, which makes it challenging to focus on the here and now or make plans for the future.

In order to establish balance between introspection, being present, and moving forward, this chapter examines how sadness warps one's perspective of time and offers helpful coping mechanisms.

Understanding Time Distortion in Depression

1.The Endless Moment

Depression can make every minute feel unbearably long, especially during low-energy or anxious states. This "endless now" often leads to feelings of stagnation.

2.The Vanishing Days

At the same time, depression blurs days and weeks, creating a sense of time slipping away unnoticed. This can foster guilt or frustration about "lost time."

3.Living Out of Sync

Depression often pulls us backward into regret or propels us forward into anxiety, making it challenging to live fully in the present.

Strategies for Navigating Time Distortion

1. Anchoring in the Present Moment
Mindfulness practices can help you reconnect with the present and create a sense of stability amidst the distortion.

Techniques:

Body Scan:
Close your eyes and focus on each part of your body, starting from your toes and moving upward. Notice sensations without judgment.

Five Senses Check-In: Pause and list:

5 things you see.
4 things you hear.
3 things you can touch.
2 things you can smell.
1 thing you can taste.

Breath Awareness:
Focus on your breath. Inhale deeply for a count of four, hold for four, and exhale for six.

2. Reframing the Past

Instead of becoming stuck in regret, use reflection as a tool for understanding and growth.

Techniques:

Memory Journaling:
Write about a past moment, focusing on what you learned rather than what you lost.
Compassionate Reframing:
Imagine you're comforting a friend in your position. What would you say to them about their past struggles?
Gratitude for Growth:
Identify one way your past has shaped your present strength or resilience.

3. Envisioning the Future Without Rushing

Balancing hope for the future with the challenges of the present requires gentle planning and optimism.

Techniques:

Micro-Goals:
Instead of setting long-term goals, identify one small action you can take each day to move forward, like reading for five minutes or taking a short walk.
Visioning Exercise:
Close your eyes and picture your future self. What small changes or comforts can you imagine adding to your life?
Daily Intentions:
Begin each day by setting one achievable intention: "Today, I will focus on eating a nourishing meal" or "I will write down one hopeful thought."

Creating a Balanced Relationship with Time

1. Building Rituals
Rituals create markers in your day, helping to establish a sense of rhythm and normalcy.

Morning coffee brewed with intention.
Evening journaling to reflect and release.
Setting a timer for small, deliberate activities like reading or stretching.

2. Tracking Time Gently

Instead of rigid schedules, use flexible tools to create structure:
The Pomodoro Method:
Work or engage in an activity for 25 minutes, then take a five-minute break.

Mood and Energy Logging:
Track how your energy ebbs and flows throughout the day to better understand your natural rhythm.

3. Reclaiming "Lost Time"

If you feel guilty about time you've "wasted," try reframing those moments as periods of rest or healing.
Consider:
What did you learn about yourself during that time?
How can you use this awareness to move forward?

Practical Exercises

1. Timeline of Resilience
Draw a timeline of your life, marking moments of struggle and growth. Reflect on how you navigated difficult periods in the past and what strengths you developed.

2. The Hourglass Visualization

Imagine an hourglass with sand flowing steadily. Envision each grain of sand as a moment of your day—passing neither too quickly nor too slowly, simply flowing as it should.

3. Daily Time Capsule

At the end of each day, write down one thought, feeling, or event. Over time, this becomes a way to track and appreciate your moments without losing them to the blur of depression.

Embracing the Flow of Time

Even while depression distorts time, it doesn't have to be your enemy. You can change how you relate to time by focussing on the here and now, thinking empathetically about the past, and gently envisioning the future.

Even while depression can cause time to bend and stretch in odd ways, these techniques serve as a reminder that meaningful moments can be reclaimed one breath, one memory, and one tiny step at a time.

Chapter 20

Becoming Whole in Your Brokenness

Resolving every scar and repairing every shattered piece is not the goal of the depressive journey till you're "perfect." It's about accepting those flaws and cracks as essential components of your identity. This last chapter celebrates the beauty of a flawed but complete life by tying together the teachings of self-discovery, vulnerability, and perseverance.

The Art of Living with Imperfections

Kintsugi, or "golden joinery," is a philosophy from Japan that provides a meaningful metaphor for living a genuine life. Gold is used to fix broken ceramics, highlighting the cracks rather than covering them up. Every imperfection serves as evidence of the item's durability and history.

What if we approached our lives the same way?

Every painful moment becomes a thread of gold in your story.
Every scar, emotional or physical, tells a tale of survival and growth.
Your imperfections are not signs of failure—they're the artistry of being human.

Seeing Life as a Mosaic

Life is a mosaic of moments, some sad, some light, all crucial to the overall scheme of things, rather than a single, flawless picture. Even though the individual parts may seem sharp, you can start to appreciate the beauty in the whole by taking a step back.

Exercises for Reflection and Transformation

1.Crafting Your Timeline of Resilience

Draw a line across a piece of paper and mark significant moments in your life.
Use gold or bright colors to highlight moments of growth born from struggle.
Reflect: What have these moments taught you about yourself?

2.Finding Beauty in Past Struggles

Write a letter to a younger version of yourself during a difficult time.

Highlight the strength and wisdom you've gained since then.
Thank your past self for enduring and paving the way for who you are now.

3.Visualizing a Mosaic Future

Imagine your future not as a straight path but as a mosaic yet to be completed.
Consider: What pieces will you gather? What colors and shapes will represent hope, joy, and acceptance?

Redefining Wholeness

Integrating all aspects of yourself—the good and the bad, the damaged and the fixed—is what it means to be whole, not to be perfect. It involves making room for paradoxes.

Strength in vulnerability.
Hope in despair.
Joy in sorrow.

Practical Tools for Embracing Wholeness

1.Daily Affirmation: "I Am Enough as I Am"

Begin each morning with this affirmation. Let it serve as a reminder that perfection is not a requirement for worthiness.

2.Golden Repairs Journal

Dedicate a journal to moments of struggle and how you've grown from them. Use golden ink or highlights to emphasize these "repairs."

3.The Kintsugi Visualization

Close your eyes and picture yourself as a piece of pottery. Imagine filling your cracks with golden light, each one a reminder of your resilience and beauty.

Building a Future Shaped by Self-Acceptance

Carrying grief with you, transformed into something important, is what it means to go forward, not leaving it behind. Your journey doesn't have to be linear or finished. Every encounter in life creates a new piece of art.

Honor Your Cracks:

View your imperfections as strengths, not weaknesses.

Celebrate the Mosaic:

Find beauty in the mix of joyful and challenging moments.

Hold Hope Close:

Know that, even amidst darkness, the light of gold is waiting to shine.

Closing Reflection

Life is an act of creation—shaping, repairing, and accepting the mosaic of your existence—rather than a pursuit of perfection. Accepting that your flaws and scars are what make you special and exquisitely human is a better way to be whole than trying to heal every flaw.

As you proceed, keep in mind that you are not a riddle that needs to be solved. With each mosaic piece and golden line adding to your tale, you are a work of art in progress.

Appendix

This appendix offers additional tools, resources, and guidance to help you navigate your journey with depression and self-acceptance. These suggestions stem from personal experience and reflections and should be used as complementary practices rather than medical advice.

Acknowledging the Limitations of This Work

It's important to note that this book is not a substitute for professional therapy, medical treatment, or diagnosis. All practices and exercises shared are based on personal insights and life experiences. If you're experiencing severe depression, please consider consulting a mental health professional or reaching out to a support group.

Practices for Daily Living

Mindfulness Apps:
Headspace, Calm, or Insight Timer for guided meditations and mindfulness techniques.
Mood Trackers:
Apps like Daylio or journaling methods to chart emotions and energy patterns.

Community Support

Seek out local or online support groups for people navigating depression. Sometimes, shared experiences can foster a sense of belonging and understanding.

Author's Note

Throughout this book, I've shared my personal journey—the challenges, contradictions, and small victories that make up life with depression. While these tools have helped me, they are not universal solutions. If even one exercise, story, or reflection resonates with you, I hope it offers a small glimmer of light on your path.

A Final Reminder

"You are not alone".
"You are not broken".

Glossary

Acceptance Practices Techniques aimed at embracing emotions, situations, and imperfections without judgment, fostering self-compassion and resilience.

Anchoring in the Present Moment Mindfulness practices that help ground an individual in the current moment, counteracting feelings of being stuck in the past or anxious about the future.

Body Scan A mindfulness technique where attention is focused on different parts of the body to promote relaxation and awareness.

Boundaries Emotional, mental, or physical limits set to protect one's well-being and energy from being drained or compromised.

Compassionate Reframing The process of viewing past struggles with kindness and understanding, as if comforting a dear friend, to foster healing and growth.

Creativity as Catharsis The use of creative outlets like art, writing, or gardening as a means to process emotions and find clarity amidst struggles.

Depression's Time Distortion The phenomenon where depression alters perception of time, making moments feel prolonged or entire days blur together.

Dual Journaling A journaling method where one side of the page captures grief or challenges, while the other side reflects moments of light or hope.

Five Senses Check-In A grounding exercise that involves listing things you perceive with each of the five senses to bring awareness to the present.

Golden Repairs A metaphor inspired by kintsugi, where emotional or physical scars are seen as strengths and opportunities for growth, symbolized by gold-filled cracks in pottery.

Gratitude Practices Simple daily exercises that help individuals focus on positive aspects of life, even amidst pain, such as listing one thing they are grateful for.

Micro-Goals Small, manageable tasks that make larger goals feel achievable, promoting a sense of progress and accomplishment.

Personal Manifesto A written declaration of one's values, beliefs, and aspirations, serving as a guide for meaning and direction in life.

Pomodoro Method A time management technique that alternates focused activity sessions (e.g., 25 minutes) with short breaks to maintain productivity and prevent burnout.

Bibliography

This book is deeply rooted in the author's personal experiences and reflections, shaped by a combination of lived encounters, lessons learned, and insights gathered from various sources. The references listed below represent materials and inspirations consulted during the creation of this work, as well as concepts discovered through independent research, including ideas found on the internet and in other books.

Books and Philosophical Influences

1.Frankl, Viktor E. Man's Search for Meaning. Beacon Press, 2006. A significant influence on understanding how meaning can emerge from suffering.
2.Koren, Leonard. Wabi-Sabi for Artists, Designers, Poets Philosophers. Imperfect Publishing, 1994.
Introduced the concept of appreciating imperfection, reflected in the book's metaphors of kintsugi and resilience.

Online Resources and Articles

Mindful.org. Practical Mindfulness Techniques to Live in the Present Moment.
Provided inspiration for exercises designed to anchor readers in the present moment.

It serves not as a list of strict references but as an acknowledgment of the diverse ideas and materials that informed the journey shared within this book.

Author Biography

Ankur Raj is an undergraduate student who has poured his personal experiences and reflections into this book, weaving a raw and authentic narrative about living with depression. Drawing from his own struggles, Ankur offers a heartfelt exploration of the complexities of mental health, the paradox of happiness and sadness, and the importance of embracing imperfections.

This work is deeply personal, shaped not by medical expertise but by the daily challenges, victories, and lessons learned while navigating the often-overwhelming emotional landscape of depression. While the insights shared are rooted in his lived experience, the book also incorporates lessons gleaned from various sources, including online resources, other books, and life stories, which helped him understand the deeper truths about emotional well-being.

Ankur's journey is one of self-discovery, growth, and resilience, and through this book, he hopes to offer a comforting hand to those who may feel alone in their struggles.

You can reach the author via this email or direct message on Instagram if you have any comments or concerns about this book.
Email : rajankur2432@gmail.com
Instagram : ankurraj51